INVESTIGAT
COMPOUNDS
AND MIXTURES

SUPER COOL SCIENCE EXPERIMENTS

CHERRY LAKE PRESS
Ann Arbor, Michigan

SCIENCE
INVESTIGATION

by Charnan Simon

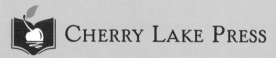

CHERRY LAKE PRESS

Published in the United States of America by
Cherry Lake Publishing Group
Ann Arbor, Michigan
www.cherrylakepublishing.com

Reading Adviser: Beth Walker Gambro, MS, Ed., Reading Consultant, Yorkville, IL

Content Editor: Robert Wolffe, EdD,
Professor of Teacher Education, Bradley University, Peoria, Illinois

Book Designer: Ed Morgan of Bowerbird Books

Grateful acknowledgment to Deborah Simon, Department of Chemistry,
Whitman College

Photo Credits: cover and title page, 4, 5, 6, 7, 8, 10, 11, 12, 15, 16, 18 left, 19, 20, 23, 24, 27, 29 freepik.com; 9, 13, 14, 17, 18 right, 21, 22, 25, 26, 28, The Design Lab.

Cherry Lake Press is an imprint of Cherry Lake Publishing Group.

Library of Congress Cataloging-in-Publication Data has been filed and is available at
catalog.loc.gov

Printed in the United States of America
Corporate Graphics

A Note to Parents and Teachers: Please review the instructions for these experiments before your children do them. Be sure to help them with any experiments you do not think they can safely conduct on their own.

A Note to Kids: Be sure to ask an adult for help with these experiments when you need it. Always put your safety first!

Note from Publisher: Websites change regularly, and their future contents are outside of our control.
Supervise children when conducting any recommended online searches for extended learning opportunities.

CONTENTS

Looking for MIXTURES!

Think of a jar of marbles. You see many colors. The marbles can be mixed in the jar in different combinations. Even so, they are not joined together in a special way. Would you believe that this jar of marbles represents something scientific? The colorful marbles form a simple mixture.

Have you ever looked for or identified other mixtures around you? Consider a bowl of cereal or mixed nuts. If so, you're on your way to thinking like a scientist! Did you know that you can carry out experiments using materials you have at home? Together, we'll learn how scientists think. We'll do that by experimenting with mixtures and **compounds**. We'll find out how mixtures and compounds are alike and different through these experiments!

Different nuts form a mixture.

Getting STARTED

Scientists learn by studying something very carefully. For example, scientists who study mixtures and compounds know that some substances mix easily and some don't. Some substances dissolve in a **solution**. And sometimes when two substances mix, there's a chemical reaction. Then a whole new substance is created!

Scientists **conduct** experiments to see how these reactions happen. Good scientists take notes on everything they discover. They write down their **observations**. Sometimes those observations lead to new questions. With these new questions in mind, scientists design experiments to find answers.

When scientists design experiments, they often use the scientific method. What is the scientific method? It's a step-by-step process to answer specific questions. The steps don't always follow the same pattern. However, the scientific method often works like this:

STEP ONE: A scientist gathers the facts and makes observations about one particular thing.

STEP TWO: The scientist comes up with a question that is not answered by the observations and facts.

STEP THREE: The scientist creates a **hypothesis**. This is a statement about what the scientist thinks might be the answer to the question.

STEP FOUR: The scientist tests the hypothesis by designing an experiment to see whether the hypothesis is correct. Then the scientist carries out the experiment and writes down what happens.

STEP FIVE: The scientist draws a **conclusion** based on the result of the experiment. The conclusion might be that the hypothesis is correct. Sometimes, though, the hypothesis is not correct. In that case, the scientist might develop a new hypothesis and another experiment.

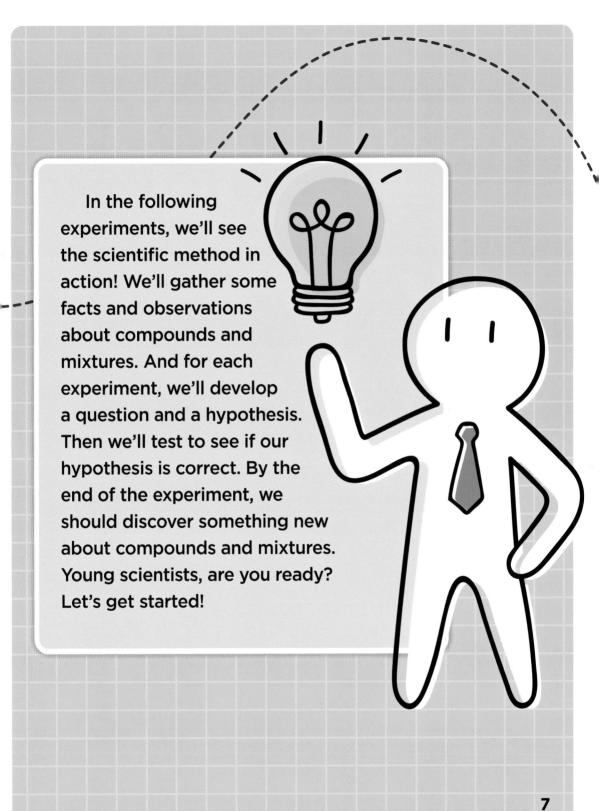

In the following experiments, we'll see the scientific method in action! We'll gather some facts and observations about compounds and mixtures. And for each experiment, we'll develop a question and a hypothesis. Then we'll test to see if our hypothesis is correct. By the end of the experiment, we should discover something new about compounds and mixtures. Young scientists, are you ready? Let's get started!

· EXPERIMENT 1 ·

Mix It Up

First, let's gather some observations. What do you already know about mixtures? You probably know the basics: A mixture is a blend of two or more substances. This observation leads us to several questions. What happens when you try to mix one substance with another? Do the two substances stay separate? Can they be unmixed? Come up with a hypothesis about separating the parts of a mixture. Here is one option: **Some substances stay separate when mixed and can be unmixed.** Now you can set up an experiment to test the hypothesis.

Here's what you'll need:

- 1 tablespoon of dried beans
- 3 tablespoons of sand
- 4 small bowls
- 1 tablespoon of small pebbles
- 1 tablespoon of salt
- 1 tablespoon each of green and red sugar sprinkles
- Kitchen colander
- Baking sheet

· INSTRUCTIONS ·

1. Pour the dried beans and 1 tablespoon of sand in a bowl. Pour the pebbles and 1 tablespoon of sand in another bowl. Add 1 tablespoon of sand and the salt to the third bowl. Pour the green and red sugar sprinkles in the fourth bowl.

2. Stir the substances to mix them together.

3. Place the colander on the baking sheet. Carefully pour the sand and beans mixture into the colander. Gently tap the colander with your hand. What happens? Does some of the sand fall through the holes onto the cookie sheet? Do the larger beans stay behind in the colander?

4. Empty the colander.

5. Pour the sand and pebbles mixture through the colander. What passes through and what doesn't?

6. Empty the colander and test the sand and salt mixture the same way.

7. Test the mixture of sugar sprinkles the same way and observe what passes through the colander.

· CONCLUSION ·

What did you notice about the four mixtures you created in the bowls? Did the substances keep their individual characteristics even after being mixed? Could you still see beans and sand, pebbles and sand, salt and sand, and red and green sugar sprinkles?

We used the colander as a tool to help us unmix the materials. Did the colander separate the substances in all four mixtures? The holes in the colander may have been too large to separate the finer ingredients. Both the red and green sugar might have been able to fall through the holes onto the baking sheet. How about the sand and salt? Depending on the type of colander, the holes might have been too big to keep the sand or other fine particles from falling through. But that doesn't mean the materials can't be separated. Can you think of different ways to separate materials that the colander couldn't? Was your hypothesis correct?

FACTS!

It would be hard work, but you could, for example, separate the sand from the salt by hand. The sand and salt haven't changed into something different. In other words, the substances making up the mixture are not chemically combined. They can still be separated.

EXPERIMENT 2

What's the Solution?

You've seen what happens when you mix solid substances together. A solution is another common type of mixture. It is made up of a solute (something that dissolves, usually a solid) mixed with a solvent (a substance, usually a liquid, that will dissolve other substances). Is it possible to add a solute such as sugar to a solvent such as water? Would this form a mixture that is **homogeneous**, or the same throughout?

Let's try it and find out! Our hypothesis will be: **The addition of sugar to water will form a homogeneous solution.**

Here's what you'll need:

- Spoon
- Drinking glass
- Dishwashing liquid
- Water
- Paper towel
- Distilled water
- 1 teaspoon of sugar
- Drinking straw

· INSTRUCTIONS ·

1. Wash the spoon and glass in soapy water. Rinse them, and then dry them with a paper towel.

2. Fill the glass halfway with distilled water.

3. Add the sugar and stir until no particles can be seen.

4. Set the drinking straw in the sugar water. Hold your finger over the top of the straw as you raise it out of the glass (this will keep the mixture in the straw). Taste the liquid. Remember how sweet it tastes.

5. Use the straw to taste samples from the bottom, middle, and top of the glass. Compare the taste of the mixture samples.

· CONCLUSION ·

Do the samples all have the same level of sweetness? Does this mean the solution is evenly mixed?

The solute (sugar) in your solution has dissolved in the solvent (water). The sugar has broken apart into smaller and smaller particles. These particles spread out evenly in the water. The mixture is homogeneous because the sugar molecules and the water molecules are evenly mixed. The samples in your straw contained the same proportion of sugar molecules to water molecules no matter where in the solution they came from. This solution is still a mixture. The sugar molecules and the water molecules have not combined chemically to form a new substance. Was your hypothesis correct?

What would happen if you added more sugar solute to your solution? A solution that will not dissolve any more solute is saturated.

FACTS!

Did you know that solutes don't have to be solids? Solutions can also be gases dissolved in other gases and liquids dissolved in other liquids. If you mix things and they stay in even distribution, it's a solution.

· EXPERIMENT 3 ·

Suspend It!

Water is known as the universal solvent. It can dissolve more solutes than any other liquid. Does this mean that water dissolves all solutes? Here are two possible hypotheses:

Hypothesis #1: All solutes can be dissolved in water.

Hypothesis #2: Some, but not all, solutes can be dissolved in water.

Here's what you'll need:

- Tablespoon
- 3 clear jars, with lids, that are the same size
- 2 tablespoons of soil
- 2 tablespoons of flour
- 2 tablespoons of salt
- Water

· INSTRUCTIONS ·

1. Put 2 tablespoons of soil in a jar. Put 2 tablespoons of flour in the second jar. Add 2 tablespoons of salt to the third jar.

2. Fill each jar with water and screw the lids on tightly. Shake each jar 10 times.

3. Put the jars on a tabletop. Let them sit undisturbed for 30 minutes. Observe the contents of the jars every 5 minutes.

Soil

Flour

Salt

CONCLUSION

What happens in each jar? The salt dissolves in water. But as soon as you stop shaking the other two jars, gravity starts pulling the soil and the flour down. The heavier soil particles settle first. The smaller flour particles take longer. Both substances are eventually pulled to the bottom of the jars. To really see this in action, observe your soil and flour jars again after 2 hours. Has the water become very clear?

Did you prove your hypothesis? If you chose Hypothesis #2, you did. Water may be called the universal solvent, but it doesn't dissolve everything. Instead of three solutions, you've made one solution and two **suspensions**. The soil and flour particles spread out, or became suspended, in the water for a while. They eventually settled to the bottom of the jar.

FACTS!

Don't worry if you chose Hypothesis #1, which turned out to be wrong. Sometimes scientists are wrong. They must repeat their experiments over and over to make sure they get the same results. Scientists want to be absolutely sure that the hypothesis is correct—or incorrect! There is no failure in science. Every finding, right or wrong, teaches us something new.

Bring Back the Substances!

A mixture is a blend of two or more pure substances (**elements** or compounds) that are not chemically combined. The mixture can usually be separated into the original components by physical means. You saw one way to separate two solid components of a mixture in Experiment #1. Can you also separate substances combined in a solution or a suspension? What do you think?

Here is one hypothesis you might want to test: **Because solutions and suspensions are mixtures, the materials combined in them can be separated.**

Here's what you'll need:

- 2 tablespoons of flour
- 2 tablespoons of salt
- Clear drinking glass, washed and dried
- Clean spoon
- Warm tap water
- Coffee filter
- Wide-mouthed jar
- Rubber band
- Shallow dish

· INSTRUCTIONS ·

1. Add the flour and salt to the glass. Stir well.

2. Fill the glass with hot tap water. Stir well. Let the glass sit for 20 minutes.

3. Collect a spoonful of the water and taste a bit of it. What happened to the flour?

4. Put the coffee filter over the top of the jar. Hold the sides of the filter in place by stretching the rubber band over the mouth of the jar.

5. Stir your water mixture to put the flour back in suspension. Slowly pour some of the liquid onto the filter. What happens? Record your observations.

6. Pour some of the liquid that passes through the filter into the shallow dish. Set the dish on a sunny windowsill until all of the water disappears. This may take several days. What do you see in the dish once all of the water is gone?

·CONCLUSION·

Were you able to separate the parts of a solution and suspension? Was your hypothesis correct?

During Step #2, the salt dissolved in the water to form a solution. That's why the water at the top of the glass tastes salty. The flour stayed suspended in the water for a while. It eventually settled to the bottom of the glass. The particles in a suspension are too large to fit in the spaces between the molecules of water. They settle when the mixture sits. You've created a solution and a suspension in one glass!

Is a coffee filter an effective way to separate the mixture? The flour particles are too large to pass through the filter. The salt particles are small enough to pass through the filter, however. Using filters is one physical way of separating the parts of a mixture. The water in the solution you placed near the sunny window should have evaporated. Evaporation is the process in which a liquid changes to a gas or vapor. The salt crystals are left behind in the dish. Evaporation is another physical way of separating a mixture.

Your hypothesis is correct! You've separated out the original substances that made up your solution and suspension.

· EXPERIMENT 5 ·

Compound the Fun

So far, we've done experiments with various types of mixtures. Now it's time to investigate compounds. A compound is a combination of two or more elements. Unlike a mixture, a compound is formed by a chemical reaction on the molecular level. The resulting compound is a completely new substance. It cannot be changed back to its original elements by simple physical means.

There are many different kinds of chemical reactions. This experiment will combine two substances to create a familiar chemical reaction. Do you know what happens when vinegar and baking soda come together? Many students know to use this combination to make a homemade volcanic eruption, but there is more going on than you might think. Our hypothesis: **A chemical reaction will take place when baking soda is combined with vinegar, resulting in a new substance.**

Here's what you'll need:

- Safety goggles
- Red food coloring
- 1 cup of white vinegar
- Funnel
- 1 tablespoon of baking soda
- Small plastic bottle
- Large tray
- Dirt, sand, and gravel

· INSTRUCTIONS ·

1. Put on your safety goggles. Add 5 drops of red food coloring to the cup of vinegar.

2. Use the funnel to pour the baking soda into the plastic bottle. Place the bottle in the middle of the tray.

3. Pile dirt, sand, and gravel around the bottle. You are forming the cone of your volcano. Leave the opening of the bottle uncovered, and be careful not to spill dirt in it!

4. Use the funnel to quickly pour all of the colored vinegar into the bottle. What happens next?

·CONCLUSION·

Did your volcano erupt? Did a bubbly or frothy mixture ooze out? What could have caused the change in your materials? Did you prove your hypothesis?

You might have been able to hear a faint hissing sound as the baking soda and vinegar came into contact with each other. The baking soda reacts chemically with the vinegar. In the process, a new substance is produced: carbon dioxide gas. This gas builds up enough pressure inside the bottle to force the red liquid out the top. The mixture of gas and liquid produces the foam.

FACTS!

One way to help you better understand compounds is to think of a cake. The cake's ingredients are all mixed and combined. Pretend these ingredients are elements. When a cake comes out of the oven, does it look like the component elements? Have changes taken place that would make it difficult to turn that cake back into the original ingredients?

·EXPERIMENT 6·

Do It Yourself!

You might have heard someone say, "Those two are like oil and water!" The person was probably talking about two people who don't get along. Is there some science behind that expression?

Scientists know that some liquids are **immiscible**. In other words, they do not mix. Instead, they separate into layers. Other liquids are **miscible**. They can be mixed. Do you think cooking oil and water are immiscible liquids? Come up with a hypothesis. What would you need to run an experiment and test the hypothesis?

An emulsion is a mixture of immiscible liquids. Scientists also know that some things can be added to emulsions to help them stay stable and mixed. These things are called emulsifying agents. They help prevent the emulsion from separating into layers.

Soap is one emulsifying agent. Did you find that oil and water are immiscible liquids? If so, would adding drops of dishwashing detergent to the mixture affect how the liquids behave? There's only one way to find out. Gather your supplies, come up with a hypothesis, and write down the steps of your experiment. Then comes the fun part. Run your own experiment and see what happens!

FACTS!

Adding emulsifying agents to some mixtures and then mixing them well can create a **colloid**. Homogenized milk is a colloid. Mayonnaise and marshmallows are colloids, too. The individual particles are still there, but they're harder to separate out. You can only see them with a powerful microscope.

Glossary

colloid (KOL-oid) a substance made of tiny particles that do not dissolve but remain suspended in a gas, liquid, or solid

compounds (KOM-poundz) substances in which elements are bound to each other in a definite ratio of each element

conclusion (kuhn-KLOO-zhuhn) a final decision, thought, or opinion

conduct (kuhn-DUHKT) to carry out

elements (EH-luh-muhnts) substances that cannot be separated into simpler substances using chemistry; the fundamental substances that make up all matter in the universe

homogeneous (hoh-muh-JEEN-ee-yuhss) uniformly the same throughout

hypothesis (hye-POTH-uh-sihss) a logical guess about what will happen in an experiment

immiscible (ih-MISS-uh-buhl) incapable of being mixed

miscible (MISS-uh-buhl) capable of being mixed

observations (ob-zur-VAY-shuhnz) things that are seen or noticed with one's senses

solution (suh-LOO-shuhn) a mixture in which the molecule-sized particles of a solute are evenly spread out among the solvent molecules

suspensions (suh-SPEN-shuhnz) mixtures in which tiny particles remain suspended in a liquid or gas without dissolving

For More Information

BOOKS

Biberdorf, Kate. *Kate the Chemist: The Big Book of Experiments*. New York: Philomel Books, 2020.

Heinecke, Liz Lee. *Chemistry for Kids*. Beverly, MA: Quarry Books, 2020.

Miodownik, Mark. *Liquid Rules*. Boston: Mariner Books, 2020.

WEBSITES
Explore these online sources with an adult:

Britannica Kids: Chemistry

PBS: Compound Basics

PBS Kids: Sorting and Mixtures

Index

About the Author

Charnan Simon is a former editor of *Cricket Magazine* and the author of more than 100 books for young readers. She lives in Seattle, Washington, and is learning more about chemistry every day.